W9-CDO-919

DISCARDED
from
New Hanover County Public Library

NEW HANOVER COUNTY
PUBLIC LIBRARY
201 CHESTNUT STREET
WILMINGTON, N C 28401

The War of the Regulation

and

The Battle of Alamance, May 16, 1771

DISCARDED
from
New Hanover County Public Library

BY

WILLIAM S. POWELL

RALEIGH

DIVISION OF ARCHIVES AND HISTORY

NORTH CAROLINA DEPARTMENT OF CULTURAL RESOURCES

Fifth Printing

1975

DEPARTMENT OF CULTURAL RESOURCES
MRS. GRACE J. ROHRER, Secretary

DIVISION OF ARCHIVES AND HISTORY
ROBERT E. STIPE, Director
LARRY E. TISE, Assistant Director

NORTH CAROLINA HISTORICAL COMMISSION
T. HARRY GATTON, Chairman

MISS GERTRUDE CARRAWAY   J. C. KNOWLES
GORDON S. DUGGER   HUGH T. LEFLER
FRONTIS W. JOHNSTON   EDWARD W. PHIFER, JR.

FOREWORD

The rise and progress of the Regulator movement and the Battle of Alamance have long been topics of interest to North Carolinians. The subject, a highly controversial one, has attracted many writers, most of whom have been sympathetic toward the Regulators and critical of Governor Tryon and the royal government. The first impartial study of the subject was made by John Spencer Bassett and was published in 1895. The present narrative, written by William S. Powell, professor of history at the University of North Carolina at Chapel Hill, seeks likewise to maintain an impartial point of view and to present the subject in a way that will be suitable for schoolchildren. It is believed that the bibliography will be useful to advanced students and that the illustrations will be of general interest. Readers who wish to undertake further research in the subject are invited to consult *The Regulators in North Carolina: A Documentary History, 1759-1776*, compiled and edited by William S. Powell, James K. Huhta, and Thomas J. Farnham (Raleigh: State Department of Archives and History, 1971).

A modern visitor center at Alamance Battleground State Historic Site, located six miles south of Burlington, features an audiovisual presentation of the story of the Regulators and the Battle of Alamance. The Alamance Battleground and the picnic area are open to the public Tuesday through Saturday, 9:00 A.M. to 5:00 P.M., and on Sundays from 1:00 P.M. to 5:00 P.M. For information about guided tours of the site, write to Alamance Battleground, Route 1, Burlington, North Carolina, 27215.

Memory F. Mitchell
Historical Publications Administrator

May 16, 1975

In 1902 this Colonial Column was unveiled at Guilford Courthouse National Military Park near Greensboro. Three plaques on
the monument commemorate the Regulator Movement; a fourth
plaque celebrates the victory at Moores Creek Bridge, February,
1776, illustrating the then-prevailing opinion that the Battle of
Alamance was the first engagement in the American Revolution.
In 1962 the monument was moved to Alamance Battleground
State Historic Site, where it is on indefinite loan. The bronze
plaques were executed by Bureau Brothers of Philadelphia.
Photograph by Larry G. Misenheimer, Division of Archives and
History.

The War of the Regulation

And

The Battle of Alamance, May 16, 1771

A great many of the people of North Carolina in the years just before the American Revolution were restless and dissatisfied with the state of affairs in their province. Their grievances were serious and affected their daily lives. Royal governors sent from outside the province were not able to maintain peace and quiet, but instead frequently gave the people further cause, fancied or real, for discontent. The outstanding group opposing the ruling class represented by the governor and his friends were known as Regulators.

The Regulators were frontiersmen allied in opposition to practices of government officials which they considered unjust and tyrannical. It was in Anson, Orange, and Granville counties in 1764 that these people first began to make themselves heard. They were called "the mob" and created a number of local disturbances until Governor Arthur Dobbs issued a proclamation forbidding the taking of illegal fees, a practice which in large measure had led to the uprising. Within four years the group was joined by others with similar grievances and they came to be known as Regulators.

The complaints of the Regulators were numerous and were based on what they considered unjust treatment received at the hands of local officials and attorneys. Most of the Regulators lived in the western or frontier counties separated from the older established eastern counties by a sparsely settled region of pine forest. They had no navigable streams and few roads linking them to the east. These new men of the west, who for the most part had come from Pennsylvania, Maryland, and Virginia, were pioneers having little in common with the easterners and practically no share in the government of the province or of their own local region.

North Carolina was a royal colony and the governor was appointed by the crown. The governor and council, which was also appointed by the crown but usually on the recommendation of the governor, formed the executive branch of the government. The governor's approval was necessary before a bill became law and he was commander of the militia. In local government he and the council appointed the county justices while he alone appointed militia officers and selected the sheriff from three freeholders whose names had been submitted to him by the county court. These factors contributed to make the governor's influence paramount.

Of the two systems of courts, superior and inferior, the former was divided into six circuits traveled twice a year by the chief justice and his two associates. Lesser officers of this court were appointed through the governor. The inferior court was the county court. It was held by the justices of the peace and was in nearly every respect the primary unit of local government. Its commands were executed by the sheriff, usually through his large number of deputies. It was the sheriff who collected the county and parish taxes levied by the county court. The clerk of this court was appointed by the secretary of state and the post generally went to the man who could pay the most rent for it.

The council made up the upper house of the legislative body while the lower house or assembly was elected by the freeholders. Elections for the assembly were conducted by the sheriff but with very little or no supervision of the polls. Influential men generally brought out a candidate and assured his election.

As a result of this system of government there was in each county a group of men which was likely to have complete control of affairs. To operate effectively the government depended too much on the personal honesty of the officeholder. Such a system seems to have worked fairly well in the eastern area, but elsewhere there is evidence that the officers were selfish and greedy and that they stuck together to further their own gain. It was in an effort to eliminate this state of affairs that the Regulator movement came into existence.

Particularly burdensome to the people of Orange County were excessive taxes, dishonest sheriffs, and extortionate fees. These evils were the more felt because of the scarcity of money; local trading was generally confined to barter. When a sudden need for cash arose it was the custom to borrow from a neighbor, who occasionally lent small sums of money. The sheriff, however, when he had come unexpectedly to collect taxes, refused to be delayed while the taxpayer went off to borrow money. Sometimes fees were charged for the delay and at other times the property would be sold before the luckless owner could secure cash and proceed to Hillsboro to pay. Many times, it seemed to these people, their property was sold to some friend of the sheriff's for much less than its true value.

The sheriffs were believed to be unjust and dishonest not only in collecting taxes but also in failing to keep proper records of these transactions and to pay into the public treasury all sums received. Governor Tryon in 1767 expressed the opinion that "the sheriffs have embezzled more than one-half of the public money ordered to be raised and collected by them." For fear of defeat at the hands of the sheriffs' friends at the next election, the treasurers did not press the matter of the failure to make full returns. In 1770 after an investigation had been made it was reported that throughout the province the sheriffs were in arrears to the extent of £49,000. Several counties were in arrears for ten years and some even back to 1754. The long arrears were mostly in the counties of Anson, Orange, Johnston, Rowan, Cumberland, and Dobbs.

Perhaps of even greater concern to the frontier people were what they considered the extortionate fees required by public officials and attorneys. It has been said that "as soon as counties were organized on the frontier sheriffs, clerks, registers, and lawyers swooped down upon the defenseless inhabitants like wolves." It was suspected that superior and county court officials conspired to aid these officers in escaping punishment. In spite of the fact that lawyers' fees were fixed by statute, enforcement was a difficult matter. Generally a service for which one fee was allowed could be divided and two or more fees demanded. Both lawyers and court officials, the people believed, worked hand in hand to postpone cases that larger fees might thereby be collected.

Many people, obliged to travel from thirty to sixty miles to the seat of county government, were greatly inconvenienced by this postponement. Frequent proclamations by the governor against the taking of illegal fees had not the least effect.

The general scarcity of money contributed to the state of unrest in the whole province, but especially in the western counties. British colonial policy had the effect of draining off gold and silver while an act of Parliament, passed for the protection of British merchants, forbade the colonies to issue legal-tender paper. Petitions to the king by the assembly to remedy this situation were without avail. Distress was widespread, but in the east where there were warehouses for receiving commodities it was less evident than in the west where there were none. The easterners used the warehouse certificates as a medium of exchange among themselves.

Isolated and out of sympathy with the easterners, the people along the frontier were ripe for revolt and needed only a leader to provide the spark which would start the explosion.

Hermon Husband came nearer to providing this spark of leadership than any other man though his role seems to have been less as a leader than as a driver or agitator. He was a native of Maryland, originally a member of the Church of England but afterwards a Quaker, and a disciple of Benjamin Franklin from whom he received political pamphlets of a patriotic character which he reprinted and circulated among the people. Husband's strategy was not unlike that of Mahatma Gandhi of recent times. By means of public sentiment he sought to effect reform. When it became evident that the Regulator movement was running into violence he held aloof from it, only exerting himself to restrain excesses and to make peace. His activity as a pamphleteer, however, had given him such a reputation that it was impossible to convince the provincial government that he was not the chief leader of the popular side. Husband's pacific intents were further illustrated on the day of the battle of Alamance. He was present using his best efforts to bring about a last-minute truce when he realized that his words were falling on deaf ears. Rather than face the violence about to break, he mounted his horse and rode away.

At no time during the Regulation was there an outstanding leader. James Hunter, often referred to as the "general" of the Regulation, declined to take command after Husband's departure, saying, "We are all freemen, and everyone must command himself." Rednap Howell and William Butler were also prominent in the movement.

Poised opposite Husband was Edmund Fanning, local leader of the opposition to the Regulators. A native of New York and a graduate of Yale, Fanning represented to the Regulators all that was evil in their government. He was in their midst as an officeholder appointed by the easterners and like his associates was one who stretched his authority as far as possible so as to take more money from the people.

By far the most prominent leader of the opposition, however, was Governor Tryon, who took office in 1765 at the death of Governor Dobbs. While Tryon has generally been painted as the epitome of harsh royal governors, he seems nevertheless to have had decided executive ability, great tact, and broad ideas. It was he who persuaded the assembly to vote funds for the erection of "Tryon's Palace" in New Bern, a structure designed to serve not only as the residence of the governor and as the seat of government but also as the central storage place for the records of the province. Taxes levied for this building—known far and wide as the most beautiful in colonial America—were not least among the grievances of the Regulators. Tryon's greatest desire at the outset of his administration was for a period of peace in a hitherto troublesome colony. He came to administer the royal government and to build up his personal fortune, however, and to accomplish these ends he relied on the county officeholders.

The War of the Regulation did not spring full-grown in Orange County, but was instead the product of a series of events. It was the result of a long pent-up feeling of discontent and restlessness over existing conditions in the province and the outcome of several minor clashes at vari-

EDMUND FANNING. THE AUTOGRAPH IS FROM AN ORIGINAL LETTER IN
THE STATE DEPARTMENT OF ARCHIVES AND HISTORY, RALEIGH.

ous points in North Carolina. Outbreaks of violence during the collection of taxes in Anson County and riots in the
Granville District foretold events to follow. In May, 1765,
unauthorized settlers on a large tract of land in Mecklenburg
County rose up in arms to drive away the owner's agents
who had come to survey the land to levy quitrents. In

Granville County that same year complaint was registered over the government's "most notorious and intolerable abuses." It was not, the people stated, the "form of Government, nor yet the body of our laws, that we are quarreling with, but with the malpractices of the Officers of our County Courts, and the abuses which we suffer by those empowered to manage our public affairs." Extortionate fees and oppressive methods of collecting fees and taxes were back of these and other complaints.

An abortive effort to organize an active group to combat these evils was made in Orange County in the summer of 1766. A group of men, apparently enthusiastic over the success of the Sons of Liberty in resisting the Stamp Act, called the people to gather at Maddock's Mill to determine "whether the free men of this county labor under any abuses of power or not." Read in open court, the call was deemed reasonable and a number of officers agreed to attend. Edmund Fanning, however, termed this an insurrectionary step and no officers attended. Delegates at the meeting, therefore, were able to accomplish little. They proposed to meet annually to discuss the qualifications of candidates for the assembly, to inform their representatives of their wishes, and to investigate the official acts of officeholders. Public officials declined to cooperate, throwing all possible influence against such ideas. Discouraged over the lack of interest and support of their proposal, the leaders abandoned all efforts to secure justice through such peaceful means.

Until the spring of 1768 there were only minor clashes. Then, however, the sheriff of Orange County announced that he would receive taxes only at five specified places and for all not paid there an additional charge of 2s. 8d. would be levied. About the same time word came that the governor was going to spend £15,000 to build a residence. Opposition to these moves drew the people together into an association known at first as "the mob," but later called "the Regulation." The purpose of this group, they said, was "to assemble ourselves for conference for regulating public grievances and abuses of power, in the following particulars, with others of a like nature that may occur: (1) We will pay no more taxes until we are satisfied that they are agreeable to law, and applied to the purposes therein mentioned, unless we cannot help it, or are forced. (2) We will pay no officer any more fees than the law allows, unless we are obliged to do it, and then to show our dislike and bear open testimony against it. (3) We will attend all our meetings of conferences as often as we conveniently can. . . . (4) We will contribute to collections for defraying the necessary expenses attending the work, according to our abilities. (5) In case of differences in judgment we will submit to the judgment of the majority of our body."

The Regulators requested the sheriff and other officials to meet with them and show a list of the taxables, a statement of the disbursement of the public money, and a copy of the law establishing fees for deeds and other official papers. The officers, of course, refused and Fanning denounced the people for daring to suggest questioning them before "the bar of their shallow understanding" and attempting to set themselves up as "sovereign arbiters of right and wrong."

When feeling between these two groups was at a peak, the officers seized a Regulator's horse, saddle, and bridle and sold them for taxes. Thoroughly outraged, a band of Regulators rode into Hillsboro, rescued the horse, and before leaving town fired several shots into Fanning's house. Fanning, who was absent at court in Halifax, immediately ordered the arrest of William Butler, Peter Craven, and Ninian Bell Hamilton, leaders of the mob. He also called out seven companies of the Orange militia and made preparations to return and take personal command. Citizens of Orange were so strongly in sympathy with the Regulators that only a token force turned out equipped to fight. The officers, perhaps frightened by this turn of events, took steps towards a truce but wrote Fanning that they were simply playing for time.

The Regulators chose delegates, one of whom was Hermon Husband, not yet a member of their organization, to meet with officers to discuss their problems. But before the meeting could be arranged Fanning gathered a handful of armed men and assisted the sheriff in arresting William But-

On the important Duty of SUBJECTION to the
CIVIL POWERS.

A

SERMON

Preached before his EXCELLENCY

WILLIAM TRYON, Esquire,
GOVERNOR, and Commander in Chief of the
Province of NORTH-CAROLINA,

AND THE

TROOPS raised to quell the late

INSURRECTION,

AT

HILLSBOROUGH, in ORANGE County,

On SUNDAY *September* 25, 1768.

By GEO. MICKLEJOHN, S. T. D.

NEWBERN:

Printed by JAMES DAVIS,

M,DCC,LXVIII.

TITLE PAGE OF A SERMON DELIVERED BY THE REVEREND GEORGE MICKLE-
JOHN BEFORE GOVERNOR TRYON AND HIS TROOPS IN HILLSBORO, SEPTEMBER
25, 1768. FROM THE ORIGINAL IN THE STATE DEPARTMENT OF ARCHIVES
AND HISTORY, RALEIGH.

ler and Husband. They were charged with inciting the people to rebellion. After a trial before a justice of the peace the two prisoners were confined in the Hillsboro jail. Husband, however, was scheduled to be removed to New Bern for safekeeping.

This act on the part of the officials so enraged the people, both Regulators and non-Regulators, that the next morning 700 men turned out to go to Hillsboro to rescue the prisoners. The officials, becoming alarmed, released the prisoners in time to send them on their way to meet the approaching Regulators who were about to swarm into Hillsboro. The governor's secretary informed the people that the governor would receive their petition to investigate conditions in Orange County if they would disband and return to their homes and that Governor Tryon would see that they received justice.

Tryon, however, claimed that his secretary had exceeded his authority and he refused to deal with the Regulators as an organization but to the people he stated the amount of taxes due for 1767. In addition he promised to issue a proclamation forbidding the officers' taking illegal fees and ordered the attorney general to prosecute all officers duly charged with extortion.

In July, 1768, Tryon himself proceeded to Hillsboro in an effort to induce the people to abide by the laws. After his arrival the Regulators met to consider his reply to their demands and decided to petition the assembly inasmuch as the governor's proclamation had had little effect. Several meetings were held and the opposing factions were in frequent communication. The governor instituted proceedings against several officials, including Colonel Fanning, who was charged with extortion. The Regulators, however, felt that they were not able to see enough progress in the governor's moves and continued their agitation.

Tryon, to insure protection for the superior court when it met to try Husband and Butler, called out the militia. A great many of the people in the vicinity remained in sympathy with the Regulators, however, and it was not without some difficulty that Tryon was able to raise a force of 1,461 militiamen. This body of men was drawn from Rowan,

Mecklenburg, Granville, and Orange counties, and more than a fifth of them were commissioned officers including eight generals and seven colonels. Fanning, who was scheduled to be tried for extortion, was a colonel of the militia on duty at the court. Six others were members of the council, eighteen were members of the assembly, and numerous others held lesser posts in the government. Evidently, therefore, there was a close tie-up between the civil and military forces. A small office-holding class was in virtual control of affairs throughout the province.

To oppose Tryon's force 3,700 Regulators assembled but found themselves no match for the governor's trained forces and no attempt was made to interfere with the trial. After a day or two they dispersed.

Husband was tried and acquitted while Butler and two other Regulators were convicted and sentenced to fines and imprisonment. Fanning was found guilty of extortion on five counts and fined one penny for each offense. He resigned his position as register but subsequent investigation indicated that he was guilty of nothing worse than a misconstruction of the law.

The spirit of the Regulation in the meantime had grown in the other frontier counties. A band of some thirty men from Edgecombe attempted but failed to rescue an insurgent leader from the Halifax jail. In Johnston eighty men attacked the justice of the court but were repulsed when the justices and their friends took up clubs and met them in a field. In Anson 100 armed men who succeeded in breaking up the county court joined an oath-bound association to assist each other in resisting the sheriff's efforts to collect taxes. A group in Rowan attempting to prosecute certain officers for extortion failed because the grand jury refused to return true bills.

Having failed to secure justice in their courts, the Regulators decided to appeal to the assembly. Governor Tryon, in the summer of 1769, dissolved the old assembly and ordered the election of a new one. Orange, Anson, Granville, and Halifax counties returned their entire delegations. This assembly which met on October 23 was inclined to hear the petitions and suggestions of the Regulators but before taking action on that point passed several resolutions and drew up a petition to the crown on questions then at issue between the colonies and the royal government. Tryon was highly displeased and promptly dissolved the assembly. Almost immediately steps were taken to call a new election.

Legal remedies seemed to the Regulators very slow in taking effect. As a deliberative body the assembly was naturally slow and could not move with the speed which the impatience of the Regulators demanded. The reformer tends to be radical while the lawmaker is, or should be, conservative. This difference frequently brings on excesses in both words and deeds. Impatient over what they considered indifference on the part of the government to their grievances, the Regulators began to take violent steps which no government could refuse to combat. They broke into courts of justice, drove judges from the bench, and contemptuously set up mock courts. They dragged unoffending attorneys through the streets at the peril of their lives and publicly assaulted peaceful citizens who refused to sympathize with them.

Such steps as these compelled both the assembly and the governor to look less to the grievances of the Regulators and more to the suppression of anarchy. In September, 1770, Judge Richard Henderson was presiding over the superior court in Hillsboro when a mob of 150 Regulators, led by Husband, Hunter, Howell, and Butler, armed with sticks and switches, broke into the courthouse, attempted to strike the judge, and forced him to leave the bench. They next attacked and severely whipped John Williams, a practicing attorney. William Hooper, later a signer of the Declaration of Independence but then an assistant attorney general, was "dragged and paraded through the streets, and treated with every mark of contempt and insult." Fanning was pulled from the courthouse by his heels and dragged through the street before being brutally whipped. The mob then broke into Fanning's house, burned his papers, destroyed the furniture, and demolished the building. Many others were whipped as the Regulators rioted through the streets of Hillsboro. Windows of private residences were broken and the inhabitants of the town were terrorized. Court was adjourned when Judge Henderson was not able to keep order.

Such outrages created general panic among the Orange County officials and they were quick to demand a special session of the assembly. Tryon summoned his council for advice and it was decided to call the militia into active service at once. News reached New Bern of the burning of Judge Henderson's home and stables in Granville County and it was rumored that the Regulators were gathering in force to march on New Bern to overawe the assembly which met on December 5, 1770.

Despite their terror, or perhaps because of it, the assemblymen set about drawing up a series of reform measures. Acts were passed dealing with the appointment of sheriffs and their duties, fixing attorney's fees, regulating officers' fees, providing for more speedy collection of small debts, and erecting the counties of Wake, Guilford, Chatham, and Surry, all in the region in which the Regulators were numerous. Each of these laws, as well as others passed at the same time, was in line with the demands of the Regulators. While the assembly was taking this course of action, however, word came that the Regulators had assembled in Cumberland County ready for the march to New Bern. A complete about-face in the assembly resulted and thoughts were turned to the adoption of punitive measures.

To cope with the situation the assembly adopted an act generally known as the "Johnston Act," introduced by Samuel Johnston, later a member of the Continental Congress and Senator from North Carolina to the First Congress of the United States. This act, to be in force for a year, provided that the attorney general might prosecute charges of riot in any superior court in the province. All who avoided the summons of the court for sixty days were declared outlaws who were liable to be killed with impunity. In addition to these drastic steps the governor was authorized to employ the militia to enforce the law.

The Regulators reacted with defiance. In order to extend and strengthen their organization they sent messengers into Bute, Edgecombe, and Northampton counties to encourage and organize those who would join them. The people of

A Drawing of a Later Date, Depicting Governor Tryon and a Group of Regulators.

Rowan denounced the "Johnston Act" and swore they would
neither pay fees nor allow any judge or king's attorney to
hold court there. They threatened death to all clerks and
lawyers who came among them and declared Fanning an
outlaw whom any Regulator might kill on sight.

In March, 1771, Governor Tryon ordered a term of
superior court held at Hillsboro, but the judges filed a formal protest with the governor's council because, under the
conditions existing in that part of the province, they could
not hold court with any hope of dispatching business. And,
too, they feared for their own personal safety.

The council decided that the time had come for the government to take a stand against the lawless factions in the
province. They advised Tryon to call out the militia and
to march against the Regulators "with all expedition." The
law-abiding elements of the colony, who were tired of the
reign of violence, lawlessness, and terrorism which had
come with the Regulators, greeted this advice with joy.

The Regulators, however, protested to the governor tell-
ing him that they had resolved, in case he should come
among them with the militia, that every man would take
his horse from his plow and meet the governor's force. If
he came to "suppress all the disturbers of the public peace
and to punish according to their deserts the original offend-
ers in government," by which they meant the local officials
in the government, then they would join him, otherwise they
were ready to oppose him.

Tryon paid not the least heed to this protest. On March
19 he called for volunteers for the militia and when enlist-
ments were slow he offered a bounty of 40s. The bounty
had its effect and on April 23 the troops got underway.
Swivel guns, flintlocks, ammunition, and other equipment
for these troops had been sent at Tryon's request from Fort
Johnston on the Cape Fear.

General Hugh Waddell had already been ordered to march
with the Cape Fear militia to Salisbury to overawe the
Rowan Regulators, to enlist the support of the western
militia, and to march on Hillsboro from the west.

At Johnston Court House troops from Craven, Carteret,
Orange, Beaufort, New Hanover, Onslow, Dobbs, and

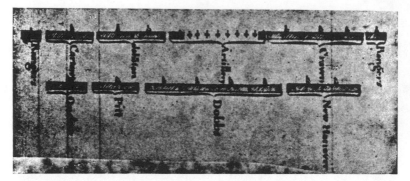

ORGANIZATION OF THE MILITIA, MAY 3, 1771, AT SMITH'S FERRY NEAR JOHNSTON COURT HOUSE FOR A FORMAL REVIEW BY THE GOVERNOR. FROM TRYON'S ORDER BOOK IN THE STATE DEPARTMENT OF ARCHIVES AND HISTORY, RALEIGH.

Johnston were joined by the Wake militia and on May 3, 1771, at Smith's Ferry nearby, Tryon reviewed his troops before breaking camp and proceeding towards Hillsboro. There were 1,068 men with Tryon and of this number 151 were officers. General Waddell, approaching Salisbury from the Cape Fear, had in his command 236 men and 48 officers coming mostly from Anson, Rowan, Mecklenburg, and Tryon counties.

On May 9 the governor and his troops arrived in Hillsboro. General Waddell on the same day left Salisbury but just after crossing the Yadkin was met and stopped by a large body of Regulators. The general called a council of officers and it was decided that in view of the numerical superiority of the enemy, and because their own men could not be relied on to fire on them, it would be wise to fall back to Salisbury.

About this time nine young men among the Regulators, later known as "The Black Boys of Cabarrus," disguised themselves and attacked a convoy that was taking some powder from South Carolina to General Waddell. They beat off the guards and burned the powder.

Tryon on May 11 left Hillsboro intending to go to the rescue of Waddell. His route was to take him through the heart of the Regulators' country and so for the sake of justice and discipline, or for policy, he issued strict orders against the taking of property by his soldiers. On the fourteenth they reached the banks of Alamance Creek where they rested for a day. On the morning of the sixteenth Tryon ordered his army of something less than 1,000 men and officers into battle formation with the companies from Carteret, Orange, Beaufort, New Hanover, and Dobbs, plus his artillery, in the lead, followed by companies from Onslow, Johnston, and Dobbs. With these troops Tryon set out to find the enemy who were assembled about five miles farther on. Two companies from Orange had remained in Hillsboro and a small contingent of troops kept guard over the camp at the Alamance.

The Regulators, estimated to have been about 2,000 in number, had gathered in front of Tryon. They lacked adequate leadership, a clear purpose, efficient organization, and even sufficient arms and ammunition for a battle. Their chiefs seemed to have felt that simply by making a display of force they could frighten the governor into granting their demands. Among their group was a number of restless and noisy individuals and many who seemed not to realize the seriousness of the situation. These, against the wishes of their leaders, captured Colonel John Ashe and Captain John Walker of the governor's troops on the morning of the fifteenth while they were out scouting and, after severely whipping them, made them prisoners. The great body of the Regulators was opposed to such action and even threatened to give up the cause entirely if such acts were repeated.

On the same day, the Rev. David Caldwell came among the Regulators in the interest of peace and went from them to Tryon in an effort to bring the opposing forces to terms. He was promised a reply the next day and as Tryon's men began to move out of camp on the sixteenth it was sent. It offered no compromise, but instead required the people to submit to the government and disperse. Tryon gave them an hour in which to comply. After delivering the message Caldwell returned to the governor in a last effort to prevent an outbreak, but without success. He went back to the Regulators and advised them to abide by the governor's orders, but they stood fast. Husband, who also had been present in the role of peacemaker, realizing

A Proclamation Issued by Governor Tryon, May 24, 1771, Urging the Regulators to Surrender Their Arms and to Accept a Pardon. Manuscript in The State Department of Archives and History, Raleigh.

the hopelessness of the situation, mounted his horse and quietly rode away.

So careless were the Regulators, and so unaware of the pending danger were most of them, that quite a few were frolicking and wrestling when an old soldier who happened to be among them warned them to expect an attack at any minute. It was very soon afterwards that the firing began.

Tryon considered the Regulators, so long as they remained under arms, to be in "a state of War and Rebellion." Consequently he could not negotiate with them and could only endeavor to restore order by whatever means seemed most sure to promise success. He gave the Regulators a choice— to return peacefully to their homes or to be fired upon. They had one hour to decide. After the hour was up Tryon sent an officer to receive their reply. "Fire and be damned!" was their answer. The governor then gave the order, but his men hesitated. Rising in his stirrups, he shouted, "Fire! Fire on them or on me!" The militia obeyed, the Regulators responded in kind, and the battle of Alamance was on.

The Regulators were no match for Tryon's well-trained and well-equipped troops with their drums beating and red silk colors flying. His officers wore yellow cockades as a readily-identifiable badge of authority, while the Regulators had no officer higher than captain and each individual company was operating independently of the others. Tryon's artillery fire was very effective in the beginning, but some of the hardy frontiersmen soon crouched behind rocks and trees and succeeded in driving away the artillery gunners and even in capturing one of the guns. These bold Regulators, however, were not supported by their comrades, most of whom had early taken leave of the field of battle.

The battle of Alamance lasted two hours. Tryon's forces lost nine killed and sixty-one wounded while the Regulators lost the same number killed and a large but undetermined number of wounded. Tryon took about fifteen prisoners of whom one was executed on the spot with the idea of striking terror to the hearts of the Regulators. This drastic step, however, was uncalled for as the "rebellion" was already crushed by the military defeat.

Tryon had the wounded Regulators treated by his own surgeons and the day following the battle issued a proclamation offering with a few exceptions to pardon all those who would submit to the government and take an oath of allegiance.

On May 21 the governor and his troops marched to Sandy Creek, an early center of the Regulator movement, where they remained a week collecting supplies and administering the oath of allegiance to those who took advantage of the governor's proclamation. On the twenty-ninth they moved westward and were joined on June 4 by General Waddell and his troops. After visiting the Moravian settlement they turned on the ninth and marched to Hillsboro where the prisoners taken at Alamance were tried before a court-martial. Six were condemned to death and executed near Hillsboro; the remainder were pardoned by the British government at Tryon's request. On June 8 Waddell departed to return to the Cape Fear by the same route he had followed in coming up. Tryon, who had just received an appointment as governor of New York, departed at once for New Bern leaving Colonel Ashe in charge of the militia with orders to return to New Bern.

Josiah Martin, who succeeded Tryon as governor, found the Regulator movement crushed when he came to take office. By July 4 over 6,000 persons had taken the oath of allegiance and in the election of 1771 the people of Orange County chose two strong anti-Regulators to represent them in the assembly. Most of the outlawed leaders of the Regulators were in hiding.

In 1772, after the expiration of the provisions of the "Johnston Act" which had been passed to be in force for one year only, the leaders of the Regulators, no longer "outlawed," surrendered and posted bond for their appearance in the Hillsboro court. Since they were not now outlaws, some other charge, as for example treason, had to be made. This discouraged further prosecution of the suits, and so far as the courts were concerned the matter stopped there. When the Revolution was beginning, the crown had the

A Drawing of the Battlefield at Alamance About 1853.

governor pardon all save Husband who had been involved in the Regulation.

The Regulators' attempt to secure reform in local government thus failed most surely. The people had either to submit or move farther into the wilderness. This great numbers of them did, some going into Tennessee and others to Kentucky after Daniel Boone, employed by Judge Richard Henderson, returned with glowing reports of that region. By 1772 about 1,500 had left and others were waiting only to sell their land before joining them.

The importance of this battle and its proper place in our history have long been topics of serious discussion not only in North Carolina but throughout the nation.

Although the spirit which motivated the Regulators was similar in many respects to that which drove the colonists to revolt against England, it did not find such clear and idealistic expression. Theirs was a local problem which required a local solution. No theory of government was involved and therefore the War of the Regulation which culminated in the Battle of Alamance must be regarded as one of the preliminary thrusts before the Revolution while the people and the colonial officers were trying to adjust the demands of the masses to the requirements of the government.

Of broader significance, the Regulators and the battle of Alamance must be cited by students of the revolutionary movement in eighteenth-century America as illustrating the dissatisfaction of a large group of people even several years before the final break at Lexington and Concord. Their boldness in taking up arms against royal authority contributed, by example, to the later clash which resulted in American independence.

At the same time the Regulator movement must also be viewed as one of a series of clashes between east and west. This uprising followed Bacon's Rebellion in Virginia by nearly a hundred years, but preceded Shay's Rebellion (1786-1787) in Massachusetts and the Whiskey Rebellion (1794) in Pennsylvania. Many of the Regulators, both before and after their defeat at Alamance, joined and enlarged

On the Alamance Battleground site is an authentic reproduction of a half-pounder cannon of the type used by Governor Tryon's militia. The Alamance Battleground marker can be seen in the background. Photograph by Larry G. Misenheimer, Division of Archives and History.

the stream of easterners moving into the west—now Tennessee and Kentucky.

It was outside the province of North Carolina, however, that the Regulator movement had one of its greatest effects. In Pennsylvania and Massachusetts where the people were on the verge of revolution the press gave lurid pictures of the struggles of oppressed North Carolinians. Sympathy was aroused and feelings were stirred up, all of which added to the growing movement which soon led to the American Revolution.

On the other hand, when the final break did come many of the leading North Carolinians in the struggle for independence were those who had fought or at least sided with Governor Tryon. Tryon's troops, after all, had been militia from North Carolina and not royal troops from England.

The real significance of the Regulators' struggle and the Battle of Alamance lies in the fact that it stood as a grand object lesson to the people of the whole country. It set them to thinking of armed resistance and showed them how weak might be the British effort to suppress a full-scale revolution. The North Carolina troops, at least, were able to appreciate the feelings of such an army. Tryon's two campaigns served to develop the military organization of the province and when the Revolution began only a call was necessary to send the army on the march. It was thus that the brilliant Whig victory at Moore's Creek was secured with the result that the most loyal section of the South was kept from joining the British and thus opening a way to cut off from the rest of the country the three southernmost colonies.

BIBLIOGRAPHY

This bibliography is not intended to be exhaustive. Manuscript material in the three leading depositories in North Carolina is described in some detail, but the printed material listed is intended only to suggest further reading on the subject.

I. *Primary*

A. Manuscript

Department of Archives and History, Raleigh.

"WAR OF THE REGULATION, 1768-1773."

This is a miscellaneous collection of approximately 300 items. It consists of financial accounts and receipts; pay-rolls; enlistment records; pension claims, provisions returns; depositions made in defense of Husband; various petitions; returns of troop strength; and order books of Waddell and Tryon, one of which contains a manuscript map of Tryon's camp and the battlefield at Alamance and a sketch showing the position of Tryon's troops when drawn up for review at Smith's Ferry near Johnston Court House, May 3, 1771. Included also are a photocopy of an account of conditions in North Carolina from the *Connecticut Journal and New Haven Post Boy*, December 3, 1773, and a typed copy of an account on the same subject from *The Boston Evening Post*, November 12, 1770.

"LEGISLATIVE PAPERS, 1689-1927."

Of the many hundreds of items in this record group approximately one-third of those for the period 1768-1771 bears in some degree on the problem of the Regulators. Of interest are such papers as petitions from citizens asking that new counties be organized in the frontier region where they had to travel great distances to the seat of local government; acts establishing fees to be allowed local officials; legislative committee reports on various questions; claims for the payment of troops and for service rendered by private citizens in defeating the Regulators; claims and petitions for pensions from the wounded and the widows of the dead among the governor's troops at Alamance; an address of Tryon to the legislature on the subject of the Regulators; testimony given in 1770 before the House by the sheriffs of Anson and Orange counties with respect to the action of the Regulators in their counties; various papers pertaining to the currency problem; orders concerning Fort Johnston, its troops, and supplies; and numerous petitions from the citizens of Orange, Rowan, Anson, and Granville counties.

"GOVERNOR'S PAPERS, 1694-1948."

William Tryon, 1765-1771. Approximately fifty items relate to the Regulators. Included are requisitions and receipts for supplies; militia orders and reports; the governor's order book for the 1768 expedition to Orange County; a petition from citizens in the region under the domination of the Regulators asking for protection and relief; various reports on the activity of the Regulators; and a list of militia officers in each of the counties.

Josiah Martin, 1771-1775. About a dozen items pertain to the Regulators. There are several character affidavits for men suspected by the governor of being connected with the Regulators; petitions concerning some of the "outlawed" Regulators; and a proclamation against excessive fees.

"GOVERNORS' LETTER BOOKS, 1764-1897."

William Tryon, 1764-1771. This volume has 295 pages of letters written by Tryon between 1764 and 1771. Many of the letters deal in some degree with the problem of the Regulators. A portion of the book, 165 pages, contains the minutes of the council, 1765-1771.

"GOVERNOR'S OFFICE, 1754-1939."

Proclamation Book. William Tryon, 1766-1771; Josiah Martin, 1771-1775. This book, consisting of 116 pages, contains copies of the proclamations of both Tryon and Martin. Many of the proclamations pertain to the Regulators as a group while others deal with the individual leaders.

Commission Book, 1761-1773. This book, consisting of seventy pages, contains commissions issued by Governors Dobbs, Tryon, and Martin for posts in the civil government as well as in the militia. Tryon's commission as governor of North Carolina is also included. Charters for the new counties of Guilford, Surry, Chatham, and Wake are also given.

Manuscript Collections, Duke University Library, Durham.

"GEORGE BANCROFT PAPERS, 1845-1861."

Consisting of fifteen items, this collection contains typed copies of letters from Bancroft to David L. Swain, president of the University of North Carolina. Among other topics, this material relates to the Regulators, Tryon, Husband, and Fanning.

Southern Historical Collection, University of North Carolina, Chapel Hill.

"REGULATOR PAPERS, 1766-1775."

This collection of twenty-four items contains copies of correspondence and papers of William Butler and five original manuscripts including letters of James Hunter and John Stringer, and fragments of a letter from Tryon.

B. Printed

Boyd, William K., editor. *Some Eighteenth Century Tracts Concerning North Carolina.* (Raleigh, 1927). Includes a number of the tracts issued by Husband and a sermon preach-

ed in 1768 before Tryon and his troops by the Rev. George
Micklejohn.

Corbitt, David L., editor. "Historical Notes," in *The North
Carolina Historical Review*, III, 3 (July, 1926), 477-505.
Several articles from the *Virginia Gazette* dealing with af-
fairs in North Carolina around 1771.

Fries, Adelaide L., editor. *Records of the Moravians in North
Carolina*. (Raleigh, 1922-47). 7 volumes. Many references
to the Regulators in volumes I and II covering the period
1752-1775.

Hudson, Arthur P. "Songs of the North Carolina Regulators,"
in *The William and Mary Quarterly*, IV, 4 (October, 1947),
170-185. Many songs of the Regulators not to be found elsewhere.

Pennsylvania Journal: And Weekly Advertiser. July 11, 1771.
Contains a letter from James Hunter, dated "Orange, Nov.
23, 1770," to Maurice Moore, New Bern, setting forth the
case of the Regulators, answering a series of questions asked
by Moore, and then asking him four questions.

Powell, William S., and others, compilers and editors. *The Regulators in North Carolina: A Documentary History, 1759-1776.*
(Raleigh, 1971).

Saunders, William L., and Walter Clark, editors. *The Colonial
and State Records of North Carolina*. (Raleigh and elsewhere,
1890-1914). 30 volumes. The standard source book for early
North Carolina history.

II. *Secondary*

A. Manuscript

Johnson, Elmer D. "The War of the Regulation: Its Place in
History." Unpublished master's thesis, University of North
Carolina, 1942. 182 pp. Attempts to determine the importance
of the War of the Regulation.

London, Lawrence F. "Sectionalism in the Colony of North
Carolina." Unpublished master's thesis, University of North
Carolina, 1933. Discusses the Regulators in the east-west
controversy, pages 55-89.

B. Printed

Bailey, William H., Sr. "The Regulators of North Carolina,"
in *The American Historical Register*, III (Nov., Dec., 1895,
Jan., 1896), 313-334, 464-471, 554-567. An old but careful study
of the subject.

Bassett, John S. "The Regulators of North Carolina (1765-
1771)," in *Annual Report of the American Historical Association for the Year 1894*. (Washington, 1895). pp 141-212.
The standard work on the Regulators.

Carraway, Gertrude S. "The Regulators," in *Greensboro Daily
News*, March 28, 1926. A popular account. (Author's name
given as "Gertrude E. Carraway.")

Caruthers, Eli W. *A Sketch of the Life and Character of the Rev. David Caldwell . . . including . . . some account of the Regulation.* (Greensborough, 1842). Presents the Regulators in a very favorable light.

Fitch, William E. *Some Neglected History of North Carolina.* (New York, 1905). Strongly sympathetic to the Regulators.

Hawks, Francis L. "Battle of Alamance and the War of the Regulation," in William D. Cooke, editor. *Revolutionary History of North Carolina.* (Raleigh, 1853). Contains some interesting information on the poetry of the Regulators and prints extracts of some of Husband's pamphlets.

Haywood, Marshall D. *Governor William Tryon, and His Administration in the Province of North Carolina, 1765-1771.* (Raleigh, 1903). An account presenting Tryon in a favorable light.

Henderson, Archibald. "Document Sheds Light on Tryon's Tyranny," in *The News and Observer* (Raleigh), February 23, 1941. Reprints in full a letter from James Hunter to Maurice Moore.

Henderson, Archibald. "Life and Times of Richard Henderson," in *The Charlotte Observer*, March 16, 23, April 6, 13, 20, 27, May 4, 11, 18, 25, and June 1, 1913. A popular study of Henderson, a member of the official class in the conflict with the Regulators.

Henderson, Archibald. "The Origin of the Regulation in North Carolina," in *American Historical Review*, XXI, 2 (January, 1916), 320-332. A study of the beginnings of the conflict.

Lazenby, Mary E. *Herman Husband, A Study of His Life.* (Washington, 1940). Biographical study of Husband.

Middleton, Lamar. *Revolt U.S.A.* (New York, 1938). Contains a discussion of the War of the Regulation as one of a series of revolts in America between 1677 and 1894.

Nash, Francis. *Hillsboro, Colonial and Revolutionary.* (Raleigh, 1903). A history of the town of Hillsboro.

Raper, Charles L. *North Carolina, A Study in English Colonial Government.* (New York, 1904). A study of the organization and operation of the colonial government of North Carolina.

Swain, David L. "The War of the Regulation," in *North Carolina University Magazine*, IX, 3 (October, 1859); IX, 6 (February, 1860); IX, 8 (April, 1860); X, 1 (August, 1860). One of the earliest studies of the conflict.

Waddell, Alfred M. *A Colonial Officer and His Times, 1754-1773. A Biographical Sketch of Gen. Hugh Waddell, of North Carolina.* (Raleigh, 1890). A biographical study of Waddell containing a chapter devoted to the War of the Regulation.